DAVID BYRD

The Language of
Achievement

CHANGING LIVES ONE WORD AT A TIME

The Language of Achievement
— Changing lives one word at a time

ISBN: 978-1-936417-55-1
BUSINESS & ECONOMICS / LEADERSHIP / MOTIVATIONAL

Published by PCG Business, a division of Pilot Communications Group, Inc. 317 Appaloosa Trail Waco, TX 76712

HOW TO REACH DAVID BYRD OR TO ORDER:
www.davidbyrdconsulting.com

For everyone who wants and needs to
make it to the next level.

DEDICATION

This book is dedicated to my dear friends and clients, Mrs. Debbie George Fritz and Mr. Ray Fritz, whose influence and genuine spirit have been instrumental in providing the inspiration for its production.

CONTENTS

INTRODUCTION

Words have power, but only when used in a common, shared context!

Without a common context, a word can be interpreted by a thousand people a thousand different ways. But when the same group becomes aware of the common, shared meaning and context of that word, the developmental power of language begins.

I've invested over 40 years in the organizational and leadership development field and now, in my later years, I enjoy working with individual clients. I work with leaders and their organizations in a system of personal management and achievement that I call The Next-Level Achievement System®.

I first became aware of using shared context as a development tool from observing a long-time client of mine. I have known this client as a friend for over 9 years and worked with her, as a client, for a little over two years. I noticed that she was doing something special that, on the surface, seemed routine. However, I began to notice the momentum being created from her efforts. She called it "The Word for the Day."

She began to host an open conference call for her organization once per week and made it completely voluntary. Each week she would choose one word from the The Next-Level Achievement System®, which was the system that she was introducing to her organization. She would discuss the meaning of the word and have one or two people on the call comment on what the word meant to them. She kept the call short, usually only 15 minutes. Eventually she delegated the responsibility of the call to others who followed the same format for the call.

When she first told me about her call, I was silently skeptical because I thought that it was being used as merely an inspirational tool, and my experiences with inspirational tools is that they soon lose all momentum.

I must admit that I was dead wrong!

What I observed after a period of six months was that the call was gaining momentum and not declining. Most importantly, I began to hear of life-changing growth from various members of this ever-expanding group of people. I heard stories of some who would come on the call without identifying themselves only to later become some of the most vocal leaders of the call.

That is indicative of a development process, not an inspirational tool!

Most people do not know how to manage the consistency of doing the right things on a daily, moment-by-moment basis

The awareness generated from this experience is the very purpose of this book. I would like to share this awareness with you in a way that helps you, as a leader, become more effective at helping people grow, which in my opinion is the number one responsibility of a leader.

This book is presented in three parts. Part one discusses some of the basic points that I wrote about in my best-selling book *The Tripping Point in Leadership*. In that book, I discussed my observations from over 30 years of experience of how apathy affects all of us. In fact, I believe that apathy is a natural, human instinct.

Think of it this way. Self-preservation is a fundamental instinctive response. So, instinctively we associate "sameness" as security. We do so because instinctively we can't interpret the difference between a real versus an imagined threat. Positive growth requires change and change represents an imagined threat to our natural, human instincts. Yes, we instinctively fight the changes required for our own positive growth.

That is why habits are hard to change, weight is hard to lose, and addictions are hard to break. We instinctively fight positive growth.

If we are unaware of this psychological response, we assume that we can cause positive change by striving to become more disciplined. I must admit that I have seen people do that. But it is most difficult, and I have found the process of increased, organizational discipline to be a never-ending, uphill climb that fails in the end.

My observations have demonstrated that the development process required for positive change and growth is best accomplished through helping people learn how to manage the power of choice on a daily basis.

I believe that you learn how to win by winning. But we have instinctively learned to treat positive growth as a discipline that you learn by setting yourself up to lose, and through losing you will eventually learn how to win. It may sound good as an inspirational battle cry, but my 40 years of experience tells me that it just doesn't work!

Part one of this book will address one of the answers to learning how to set yourself up to win. The power of choice is one of the keys, and part one will show you how to manage the three big choices that will determine the degree of your future achievement.

Part two will give you a summary overview of The Next-Level Achievement System®. This system has been proven over time with thousands of clients. This system helps people learn how to set themselves up to win and through winning, even in the smallest ways, they can grow to higher levels of achievement.

It's difficult if not impossible to effectively manage achievement instinctively! For consistent achievement to take place, you need a personal management system to help you by-pass your natural, human instincts. A system keeps you proactive at life rather than being instinctively reactive to life.

When you are set up for effective achievement, success becomes a natural by-product.

When you think about it, you can either proactively make daily choices related to your desired future, or you can instinctively react to life and allow life to decide your future for you. The personal management system helps you to become proactive at life!

Part three of this book is a glossary of words, definitions, and descriptions of their meanings. These words are foundational to The Next-Level Achievement System® and are the words that my friend uses in her "Word for the Day" call. As I said in the beginning of this introduction, words have power, but only if there is a common and shared context.

After reading this book, my sincere hope is that you may develop a new level of awareness of the value of managing the power of choice on a consistent daily basis. Also, as you learn the The Next-Level Achievement System®, my hope is that you would choose to implement this system of personal management.

Ultimately, I hope, as you become aware of the importance of being proactive at life, that you too can begin using the development process of "The Language of Achievement."

— David Byrd

PART I

PART I

CHOOSING TO SUCCEED

How many times have you heard that success is a choice? We all have, and success is a choice ... but if we don't know what to do, how can we choose?

Chapters 1-4 focus on the very elements that make up the necessary choices for achievement and success. Upon reading those chapters, you will know exactly what to do with those future choices that lead to achievement.

CHAPTER ONE

Choice — The Foundation of Achievement

Achievement is simply the result of doing the "right things" consistently over a sustained period of time. Doing the "right things" is a direct result of your personal choice. Your future is built on the choices you make, day by day, moment by moment.

It is a **natural, human tendency** to disregard the importance of your everyday choices. I think we minimize the importance of our choices because the consequences of those choices are delayed.

> **We do not experience**
> **immediate results**
> **from most of our choices.**

If we did, we **certainly would be more selective** with our choices!

Instead, we are free to make a bad or ineffective choice and feel no immediate impact, leaving us with the impression that no harm has been done.

We have all watched superstar athletes at the heights of their careers, on top of the world, suddenly make a very bad choice that later brings down everything they have worked for. We ask, "Why did they do that?"

The answer is simple: **They thought they could get away with it.** All of us would make better decisions if there were immediate consequences to our choices.

For example, if you immediately gained 50 pounds every time you ate a single bowl of ice cream, you would never eat another bowl of ice cream again. What's more, ice cream companies would be out of business by tomorrow morning!

But that is **not** the way it works.

Here is the reality:

> You eat a bowl of ice cream and nothing happens immediately. Ice cream tastes good, so you decide to eat two bowls tomorrow, three the next day, and so on. Six months later you step onto the scales and find that you have gained 50 pounds. Your response is, "Why have I gained 50 pounds? I'm shocked!"

The 50 pounds came from your **daily choices** about ice cream. The consequences of bad choices accumulated gradually without your noticing it. You can, of course, choose to stop eating ice cream daily, and in six months, lose the extra 50 pounds.

This is an exaggerated example of how choice is directly related to long-term results, and **you should never be shocked with your results because you are in complete control.** You are not a victim. The quality of your life is all about your choices.

Your brain interprets status-quo as security.

Every day you make thousands of choices. You enjoy the freedom to choose your thoughts, perspectives, actions, and associations. **However, each choice you make in life has a consequence.** So, by filling your days with effective choices, you build a future of beneficial consequences.
What that means is this:

> **The quality of your choices**
> **will determine the quality**
> **of your life.**

The Achievement System

The foundation of any system of achievement is learning to make effective, daily choices. Surprisingly, this is a unique ability. We do not naturally possess the capacity of making consistent, effective choices!

Why?

Before we answer that question, it is necessary to understand what effective choice is. **Effective choice is defined as those choices that directly relate to your immediate goals.**

For instance, if we continue with the ice cream example previously used, the choice of eating too much ice cream simply because it tastes good is an instinctive, ineffective choice if health and weight control is your goal.

However, the choice of limiting the excessive intake of calories from ice cream is an effective choice directly related to the goal of maximizing your health. Therefore, **effective choices are goal-directed choices, not instinctive choices.** Now, back to the question first posed:

**Why do we NOT naturally
possess the capacity
to make consistent effective choices
related to our achievement?**

The answer is both simple and complex.

Your natural, human instincts have one goal for you: **your safety.** Your instincts really do not care about your goals, only about your safety and comfort. When you manage your daily activities from your natural, human instincts, your response will always be in favor of keeping you where you are.

It's natural to stay right where you are. Your brain interprets sameness or status-quo as security.

In short:

your instincts are fighting **AGAINST** your achievement because achievement always involves **CHANGE** and growth, both of which are **CONTRARY** to sameness.

This means that you are undermining your own success and achievement ... naturally!

To achieve, you must first learn to **intentionally manage your process of making effective choices,** and that process must be systematic rather than instinctive.

16

This works because ...

> **A systems approach to**
> **achievement bypasses**
> **your natural instincts.**

Read that a few times to let the words digest.

I have worked with clients who have spent their entire lives managing achievement instinctively with sporadic results. On the other hand, I have watched over-whelming results from leaders who manage by a proven system of achievement.

Your instincts really do not care about your goals.

The ultimate purpose of this book is to help you understand and implement a proven system of achievement. That system begins with learning to make effective choices now, and every day. Effective choices lead to effective actions, which in turn lead to beneficial results.

If you understand this system, **you can learn how to achieve!**

Results can be directly traced back to a point of origin: **your choices!** Choice builds the foundation of your future achievement. **Your first step toward achievement is learning to make effective choices on a consistent, daily basis.** If there is such a thing as a secret to achievement, a significant part of that secret is ...

> **being aware of the power**
> **of your choices and**
> **learning to choose**
> **effectively!**

17

Qualifying factors of achievement

Sustained achievement usually depends upon certain quali-fying factors. The following is a list of four qualifying factors, along with a question for each.

By answering each of the following questions, you can deter-mine if you have the underlying, emotional foundation for sustained achievement.

> **1) Commitment to a goal** — Do I have a burning desire to achieve something specific?

> **2) Courage to persevere** — Am I willing to follow a system in developing an enhanced level of emotional courage?

> **3) Open-mindedness** — Am I willing to be coached without being defensive?

> **4) Accountable for your actions** — Will I choose to be accountable for my effective actions?

Looking at these qualifying factors, it is important to know this principle:

> **There can be no achievement
> without these characteristics
> or without a willingness to
> develop these characteristics.**

You are your own boss

I have invested over 30 years of my life in working with people in leadership positions. From my work, I have discovered that leadership skills are necessary for **everyone** and are not exclusively reserved for those who have been appointed to leadership positions.

The reality is that you are the CEO of your life!

You are responsible for your results. No one else can make the choices that you must make for your life. **Your life today represents the cumulative impact of the choices you have made, and your future will represent the sum of your choices from today forward.** You cannot change the past, but you can dramatically impact your future.

Except in extreme cases, circumstances have played a very small role in your current life position. I know this is a hard concept for some to accept, but I have found it to be true.

Culture, environment, and circumstances can dictate your future ... but only if you choose to allow it.

The truth is that culture, environment, and circumstances can dictate your future ... **but only if you choose to allow it.**

It is **still** your choice!

Some believe that if circumstances were perfect, they would be able to achieve. Others wait for the right circumstances to come along. My experience with high achievers proves the opposite. High achievers have difficult circumstances, just like everyone else, but they **consistently respond with positive actions rather than negative beliefs.**

It is your choice to become a victim of your circumstances or to respond to your circumstances with effective actions. History is filled with stories of those who have overcome unimaginable circumstances simply by choosing to do so.

Reading this book could be your first step toward building a future of your design, or you may be seeking to enhance your already successful journey. Regardless of your current position in life, your future **will always be determined** by the quality of your choices.

Notes to Self:

_____
_____
_____
_____
_____
_____
_____
_____
_____
_____
_____
_____
_____
_____
_____
_____
_____
_____
_____
_____
_____

CHAPTER TWO

MANAGING THE CHOICE OF ATTITUDE

As you know, the foundation of achievement is learning to make effective choices. Since each of us makes thousands of choices daily, it is vitally important that we make the right choices.

In all the choices you make, there are three major areas, or choice categories, that will determine the degree of your future achievement: the choice of **attitude**, the choice of **action**, and the choice of **accountability**.

We will devote separate chapters to each of these critical categories because your effective management of these three life choices **is vital to your future achievement**. In this chapter, we will discuss one of these top three choices — the choice of attitude.

Attitude is a choice!

Your management of a consistent and productive, positive attitude will determine the degree of your future achievement.

It sounds so simple, but managing a consistent, effective attitude will be one of the greatest challenges of your life. In my career, I have experienced only a few people who, in my opinion, have done an effective job at this.

Why is attitude management so difficult?

That's simple ... **FEAR!**

The emotion of fear is a protective reflex and is a basic, instinctive, human response. As an example, if you see or feel a perceived danger, your natural response is fear. **Because fear is instinctive, many people naturally develop the habit of responding to most of the circumstances of life from the emotion of fear.** Unfortunately, this leads to negative, unproductive attitudes.

Yes, negative attitudes are natural, human responses!

> Managing a consistent, effective attitude will be one of the greatest challenges of your life.

Every news channel knows that negative news tends to appeal to our natural, human instincts. That is why approximately 80% of the news reported is either negative or communicated with a negative slant. The unfortunate truth here is this:

> We are **more comfortable** with **negative news** than with **positive news.**

So, managing a positive, effective attitude is difficult because it is neither natural nor instinctive. **You must DEVELOP the capacity to manage a positive attitude.**

This leads me to my point: **We all need a systems approach to attitude management.** Without it, we will be subject to our natural, instinctive, negative thinking.

To develop a system of attitude management, you first need to understand the mechanics of how negative attitudes are developed.

Negative attitudes are instinctive

The average person develops and maintains negative thinking habits, and it all comes about instinctively!

Remember, your natural, human instincts are concerned only with your safety and comfort, and in order to keep you safe, your established habit of thinking must be maintained, and that is why the negative-thinking habit of pessimism is so common. Instinctively, **your brain interprets pessimism as a protective mechanism of security**, and your habit of pessimism is reinforced constantly.

Think of it this way:

> If you are skeptical of **everyone** and **everything**, your human instincts interpret that habit as a **safe comfort zone from all risks.**

However, the habitual perspective of pessimism will eventually become a comfortable thinking habit, and that leads to unproductive habits of thought.

In other words, you develop negative attitudes. Upon these ineffective thinking habits you begin to build "comfort zones" for yourself that impede your own growth.

Comfort zones

A comfort zone is an emotional mindset that is created from your thinking habits over a period of time. These comfort zones **misrepresent** the position of security. Your emotions interpret fear as a threat, and you then naturally retreat to your comfort zone where nothing is going to change. That status quo position is instinctively interpreted as safety.

To grow, you must develop your potential, and that potential always lies just beyond your comfort zones.

Of course, the emotional security represented by a comfort zone is an illusion. It offers no security at all, but it feels emotionally comfortable because it has been built on thinking habits that are motivated by fear.

For example, the following statements represent just a few of the more common expressions of well-established comfort zones:

"I don't trust anyone."

"I'm secure as long as I have my job."

"I don't like risks."

"If I try something new, I might fail."

"I worry about what other people may think of me."

"They have a lot of money; they sure are lucky."

Everyone has comfort zones — and you do, too. **Your comfort zones serve no purpose other than prohibiting your own growth.**

25

Here's the truth:

**You cannot grow
and be comfortable
at the same time.**

Growth feels uncomfortable because it pushes you out of your comfort zones. To grow, you must develop your potential, and that potential always lies just beyond your comfort zones.

Attitude management is imperative for every person at every level of achievement. Regardless of your level of achievement or degree of success, **there is never a position in life** where you can forget to manage your thinking habits.

Managing a positive attitude

I have heard positive attitude described as a "soft skill" and therefore not considered to be a significant factor in achievement. I strongly disagree. **Most dysfunction in business and personal achievement can be traced back to a root cause: ineffective thinking habits!**

It does not have to be that way. You can learn to manage your habits of thought and directly affect your level of performance and achievement.

Effective change always begins with awareness. People will choose to change when they are aware that the change will serve their best interest!

So, the first step in growth is becoming aware, for with an enhanced level of awareness, you can make choices that promote positive attitudes.

What is attitude?

An attitude can best be defined as a **habit of thought**. You naturally develop certain patterns of thinking about the people and world around you. These thinking habits can be conditioned and patterned by parents, friends, culture, environment, experiences, and circumstances.

If you do not assume personal responsibility for developing your own effective, positive attitudes, the world around you will shape your attitudes with average thinking, which is usually negative and unproductive. As a result, you become a victim of your own ineffective thinking patterns.

A good working definition of positive attitude is this:

> **a predetermined habit of thought dominated by faith, hope, and positive expectancy.**

The long-term result of a consistent, positive attitude is fulfillment and achievement. Without question, the long-term benefits of maintaining a positive attitude are far more desirable than the long-term effects of a negative attitude.

Every thought you entertain during the day is either positive or negative. There is no in-between or neutral thought. Every moment of your thinking pattern during the day either serves your growth or serves your stagnation.

The fastest way to promote achievement is to believe it to be possible.

Many people describe their attitude as neutral, neither positive nor negative. However, since everything in nature is either growing or decaying, there can be no neutral positions. You and your thoughts are alive and dynamic.

The thinking patterns that determine your attitudes either ...

**work to bring about your growth
or work to bring about
your decline.**

It truly is that simple!

Thoughts are creative

A positive attitude fosters creativity. Creativity cannot exist in negative thought. For example, it is impossible to discover a creative solution by thinking about all the impossibilities. **Your mind cannot entertain creativity and negative thought at the same time.**

To find a creative solution, you must think in terms of the possibilities rather than the impossibilities. The fastest way to promote achievement is to believe it to be possible. That requires the management of a consistent, positive attitude.

If you allow your natural responses of fear to direct your thinking, you personally sabotage your opportunities for achievement by choosing to quit or not to act.

Clearly, you want the long-term benefits of managing a positive attitude. We all do! Therefore, understand that **intentionally choosing to maintain an effective, positive attitude will be your most significant lesson in life.** Your daily management of the choice of attitude, on a moment-by-moment basis, is a key element in your future achievement.

The enemy of positive thought

Everyone is challenged by the emotion of fear. Fear is a

natural, human emotion that instinctively causes us to respond with a defensive reflex to any perceived threat.

If left unmanaged, **your attitudes will be controlled** by the emotion of fear.

For example, if you set a goal that requires you to do new things, these new activities will seem uncomfortable at first. That is normal, but you may instinctively respond with fearful feelings because the new activities are uncomfortable. You psychologically interpret those fearful feelings as "risks" or "dangers," while in fact these new activities may not be dangerous at all ... **but you will naturally respond with negative feelings.**

We all have a basic fear of risks and the unknown. This response is natural, yet absolutely counterproductive to achievement. **All achievement requires you to grow beyond your current status or position.**

You cannot possibly expect to grow and not confront new activities, skills, and responsibilities. If you allow your natural responses of fear to direct your thinking, you personally sabotage your opportunities for achievement by choosing to quit or not to act.

Most of the people who fail to achieve did not fail at all. They simply allowed fear to control their thinking and quit. The fear of risk and the unknown were stronger than their desire to achieve.

5 steps to mental toughness

There are five steps that will help you develop the mental toughness needed to face the challenge of your natural instinct of fear ... and to win!

STEP #1 — Maintain positive expectancy

You must keep the vision of your desired, future achievement in the forefront of your mental focus. Keep your eye on the prize! Also, recognize that fear **serves no purpose** in your personal growth unless you are actually physically threatened.

Achievement is 80% mental! **You will first accomplish your dreams in your mind before you ever realize them materially.** Being "rich" or "accomplished" is first a state of mind.

Build a vision of your future that is stronger than your fears, and fill your thinking patterns with positive expectancy.

Positive expectancy acts as a magnet. **You attract to yourself that which you set out for yourself.** Your positive expectancy actually attracts the circumstances that you will need to realize your achievement.

STEP #2 — Manage your daily choices according to your goals, not your feelings

Managing consistent, positive expectancy is difficult because you never feel the same, physically or emotionally, every single day of the week. If you only work on your goals when you feel good, **your actions will be too inconsistent to produce results.**

My long-time friend and mentor, Paul J. Meyer, would say, "Follow through with your daily plans regardless of circumstances or what other people say, think, or do."

In other words, your dreams for the future must be strong enough to keep you following through with those plans on a daily basis, no matter how you feel.

STEP #3 — *Aggressively manage your positive relationships*

Your associations with others will either promote your growth or deter it. The thinking habits of those with whom you associate affect your thinking. You must, therefore, foster relationships with people who inspire and influence your growth.

You will attract to yourself that which you set out for yourself. If you are positive and goal-directed, you will attract those of similar thinking habits.

Aggressively avoid those who impose their negative beliefs or attitudes on you. Negative attitudes create negative energy that affects all those in association. You cannot engage in negative relationships without being negatively affected, so you must manage your personal relationships aggressively!

STEP #4 — *Live in the moment!*

Life comes to each of us one day at a time. You cannot live in the future any more than you can change the past. The past is gone and tomorrow does not exist.

Many people never succeed in their life plans because they are always saying, "I'll start tomorrow." Tomorrow turns into next week, next month, and next year. Some call it procrastination, but in reality, **it is nothing more than a comfort zone.**

You procrastinate on your personal growth because it is simply more comfortable to wait. The decision to wait is most often a decision to not grow and to stay in your comfort zone.

The only part of living that really matters is right now … this moment.

31

**Living in the past
or worrying about tomorrow
is wasteful and of no importance.**

Learn to live right now! Change your thinking about waiting and develop the attitude of urgency in applying effective actions daily.

STEP #5 — Believe

Faith is a spiritual term. It makes no sense intellectually and can be understood only from a spiritual perspective. Regardless of your religious or non-religious position, belief is vital in your growth and achievement, and you cannot understand belief without an understanding of faith.

A good definition of faith is being sure of what you hope for and certain of what you do not see. You now understand why I said that it makes no sense intellectually, but faith and belief **in your potential to achieve** is vital.

Psychologists suggest that we all have three dominant parts of our being: physical, mental, and spiritual. You cannot grow and achieve without the basic belief that you can do it, and that belief involves faith. Faith requires a spiritual perspective.

Some cannot believe in anything that they cannot see or touch, but growth is always unseen until it is achieved.

There will be times in your achievement journey when quitting or giving up will seem like the only alternatives. At these times, it will take the strength of your faith to prevail. **You must believe that you can achieve, for it is the spark that sustains you.**

Managing your positive attitude

Armed with a new level of awareness of how and why negative attitudes are instinctive, you now understand why a positive attitude development program is vital to your growth, success, and achievement.

You must develop a positive, productive attitude. It will never happen naturally, **but just because it is not natural does NOT mean you cannot do it!**

Notes to Self:

_____

_____

_____

_____

_____

_____

_____

_____

_____

_____

_____

_____

_____

_____

_____

_____

_____

_____

_____

_____

CHAPTER THREE

MANAGING THE CHOICE OF ACTION

The choice of action is the second of the big three (attitude, action, accountability) life choices that form the foundation of achievement.

Let me ask you this:

> **If a key component of achievement is
> "doing the right things,"
> then what are the
> "right things"?**

The "right things" are those predetermined, effective actions that are **necessary** in achieving your goals.

Just like the choice of attitude, action is a choice, and the choices regarding your effective actions require your consistent, daily management. Every day you choose your activities. Those activities will either be effective or ineffective.

How can you determine whether an action is **effective** or **ineffective**? Simply by the end result. What you did, did it work or not? Effective actions ALWAYS **deliver desirable results!**

Effective actions

In my experiences working with high achievers, I find a common misconception regarding the choice of action. Many high achievers **overwhelm themselves** with more than they can do and then "beat themselves up" for not getting it all done.

This behavior becomes a vicious cycle of anxious, over-optimistic planning and feelings of defeat or failure.

What's interesting is that this behavior becomes a comfort zone for many! They are never satisfied because they feel they can never do enough, and this becomes a pattern of thinking and pattern of action.

Here is a key to understanding the choice of action:

> **It's not how much you do,
> but the effectiveness of
> what you do
> that really counts!**

Effective actions are those predetermined activities that support the accomplishment of your goals.

Ineffective actions, on the other hand, are those activities that tend to fill up the daily schedule but are not related to your goals. They are usually things that need to be done but are not directly related to your achievement.

For example, the dishwasher needs emptying and the car needs to be washed, but neither will advance your future vision of financial independence.

People who achieve greatly have a unique ability of separating the necessary to-do items (i.e. washing the car, balancing the checkbook, cleaning the office, etc.) **from the necessary, effective actions required to accomplish a goal.** They understand that both types of actions are necessary, but they never confuse the two in planning their day.

The underlying foundation of achievement is the consistency of your daily, effective actions.

If left unmanaged, your natural tendency is to allow your day to be managed by your fears and comfort zones. The danger of following your human instincts in choosing your daily activities is that there is no distinguishing attention paid to those actions that hold the **highest payoff.**

Effective actions always deliver desirable results!

This mindset leads you to believe that the necessary items on your to-do list are just as important as the necessary effective actions that help you reach your goals, **and nothing could be further from the truth!**

This is precisely why people choose not to do the high pay-off actions. They are instinctively drawn toward those activities that are most comfortable.

Building confidence
Admittedly, the most effective actions are usually not the most comfortable activities. And if you are working on building confidence in a new skill, what are the odds that you

will naturally choose to work on your new skill rather than choose to be comfortable?

Close to zero. And that is precisely my point! **You will not do what you need to do.**

Developing confidence in a new skill requires practicing something that you have never done before. In fact, you develop confidence from the experience of successful attempts. You try something, it works, and you have more confidence for the next attempt.

The experience is usually uncomfortable. Everything within us wants to revert back to our normal routine.

**When we experience discomfort,
we instinctively seek
to return to a
more comfortable
activity.**

Your natural, human instincts are designed to measure the quality of your comfort level and safety, not the degree of your achievement. To achieve, **you must manage your choice of action from a proven system** rather than from your feelings or emotions.

Effective actions are related to the **desired end result**, and you must always **measure your results** related to your goals.

Identifying effective actions
Not only is it essential for you to understand the effectiveness of your actions, but it is critical for you to become proficient at identifying those actions.

Within every discipline of industry or field of work, certain indicators of achievement can be identified. Those indicators are defined by the **significance of their contributions** to your success.

For example, a car dealership has the ultimate responsibility of selling cars at a profit in sufficient numbers so that the profit from total sales is greater than the overhead and payroll of operations on a monthly basis.

We can identify the "indicators of success" by first understanding that the goal of selling a sufficient number of cars on a monthly basis is the desired end result. Given the goal, we can then break the process of selling cars down into the key indicators of performance, or KPIs (key performance indicators).

Great achievers have a unique ability to separate the necessary to-do items from the necessary effective actions required to accomplish a goal.

New cars are purchased by people who are interested in a new car, have the ability to make a decision, and have the money to buy. That defines a qualified prospect.

The process of selling a car always begins with a qualified prospect, and qualified prospects are developed through a number of leads that come through a series of advertisements and call lists.

From this simple analysis, we now can identify each KPI:

> #1 — effective advertising
> #2 — call lists
> #3 — developing call lists into interested buyers
> #4 — developing interested buyers into qualified prospects
> #5 — appointments to show cars to qualified prospects

If these five KPIs are performed effectively in sufficient numbers, the end result will be car sales. This, of course, is a simplified example for the purpose of demonstration.

Any achievement goal can be broken into the key indicators of performance using this same system. When you know the right things (KPIs) that define goal-directed effectiveness, it is easier to manage your effective actions. What this means is:

> **You can now design your daily actions around the KPIs in sufficient numbers to hit your desired goals.**

As you know, achievement is the process of doing the right things consistently over a sustained period of time. In other words, with KPIs in mind, **achievement happens moment by moment, one day at a time!** When you know the right things to do, and you have identified the key performance indicators, simply exercise your power of choice and consistently do the right things.

To achieve, you must manage your choice of action from a proven system rather than from your feelings or emotions.

You now understand the significance of effective actions, how to identify the KPIs that define effective actions, and the significance of the power of choice in managing your effective actions.

Your goal now is to begin to build the habit of planning and managing your effective actions moment by moment, one day at a time, by a specific and proven achievement system.

The results will astound you!

40

Your two life choices

You only have two choices in life: **grow or decline!** There is no in-between position in life. Your human instincts will *always* direct you toward safety by consistently encouraging you to stay where you are and to not change.

If you choose achievement, you must build the habit of planning and managing your daily actions by a proven system. Your human instincts will not be sufficient.

This is no easy task, and I have found that it takes consistent practice to develop this habit. It takes approximately 90 days of practice to begin to actually see your new planning habit begin to work. **It is not easy to bypass your human instincts.** It takes constant diligence and focus to stay on track.

In developing this habit of personal management, never beat yourself up over forgetting a day here and there. That is natural and happens to everyone. When you find yourself off track and going back to your old comfort zones, stop and immediately get back to your proven system.

Measuring your effective actions

Remember that it is important to manage your effective actions in sufficient numbers to accomplish your goal. This requires that you measure your KPIs by what we call a "benchmark."

A benchmark is a time-proven standard for each KPI that, when performed at that level of activity, will produce a given degree of achievement.

Take another look at the car dealership example. The dealer must sell a certain number of cars monthly to produce the desired level of profitability. Let's say that the dealership must sell 20 cars each month to hit its goal, and from past experience the dealer knows that it takes 60 qualified prospects with a 33% closing average to sell 20 cars.

So, the benchmark for monthly qualified prospects is 60. If the dealership has 10 sales professionals, each salesperson would have a benchmark of 8 qualified prospects per month. Suppose each salesperson delivers 8 qualified prospects a month, the dealership would have a flow of 80 qualified prospects, which is more than enough to hit the goal of 20 car sales.

It takes approximately 90 days of practice to begin to actually see your new planning habit begin to work.

Using this system, you can determine the benchmark for each KPI for your own efforts. **The benchmarks must be based on experience**, and if you have no experience with your business, find someone with experience to help you determine your benchmarks.

By measuring your benchmark for each KPI monthly, you can develop a six-month rolling average. From this average, you can predict *with accuracy* your future degree of achievement.

This type of activity measurement is called a "leading indicator" of future business. Many business leaders simply measure and track monthly sales, which is what we call a "lagging indicator."

Lagging indicators track what has already happened, which means you **cannot apply any corrective actions** because the problem has already happened.

However, **by tracking leading indicators**, you have time to take corrective actions and avoid a future decline in desired results because you are measuring the *predictors* of future results.

Choosing, identifying, managing, and measuring your effective actions is the key to consistent achievement: doing the right things consistently over a sustained period of time.

Lagging indicators track what has already happened. It's too late at that point, you can't do anything about it. The answer is to track leading indicators.

Managing the choice of action is a vital part of your system of achievement.

Notes to Self:

_____

_____

_____

_____

_____

_____

_____

_____

_____

_____

_____

_____

_____

_____

_____

_____

_____

_____

_____

_____

_____

_____

_____

_____

CHAPTER FOUR

MANAGING THE CHOICE OF ACCOUNTABILITY

All of us stand at the crossroads of thousands of daily choices, but one of the most effective choices you will ever make regarding achievement is the choice of accountability.

The choice of accountability is the third of the big three (attitude, action, accountability) life choices that form the foundation of achievement.

Most people cringe whenever the word "accountability" is used. It reminds us of the time when we had to do something that we did not want to do, or the time when we had to report to someone we did not respect. **But that is not the context** of this discusion of accountability.

Accountability is motivational force

From this point on, I want you to think of accountability as **a motivational force that will push you beyond your self-imposed limitations.** And THAT is a very good thing!

Achievement is about moving to the next level of life, about doing things you never dreamed possible. To achieve, you must change, and change is adverse to our basic human instincts. This means that:

> **You must use all of your
> creative gifts of imagination,
> intuition, and choice
> to counterbalance your
> instinctive responses to change.**

Your human instincts were designed and built into your mental makeup specifically to keep you safe. It accomplishes its objective by encouraging you to seek a comfort zone where nothing ever changes.

Psychologically, your brain instinctively views growth and change **as a threat** and immediately encourages you to retreat to more comfortable activities. **That is why unproductive habits are so difficult to change!** It is also why mediocrity is the norm, and achievement is the exception.

It is important to seek an "outside-in" perspective to bring about the kind of change you need for sustainable achievement and growth. This perspective can come from a mentor or group of people with like-minded interests to whom you choose to be accountable for your goals.

The choice of accountability is usually **the most significant choice anyone can make** regarding their future achievement.

How accountability works
In making the choice of accountability, it is important to understand the mechanics of how and why it works.

You remember the simple formula for achievement: doing the right things consistently over a sustained period of time.

To make your choice of accountability more effective, you must identify the "right things," which we call key performance indicators or KPIs. At every level of achievement there are always certain activities that must be consistently performed for achievement to take place. Looking at the history of previous achievers is a good place to start.

The next step in making the choice of accountability is finding someone who has achieved at the level to which you aspire. Once you learn the right things to do from that person, **you need to discover the level of activity required to achieve your goal** within the time frame of your target date. This standard level of activity, as you know, is your "benchmark."

Now, with that understood, let's define achievement more effectively.

**Achievement is performing
all the required KPIs,
at benchmark, consistently
over a sustained period of time.**

That is how you achieve — you **choose to be accountable to your desired level of KPIs at benchmark**. That is the key to your effectiveness.

The 3 parts of accountability

There are three parts of accountability that seem to hold true. The following describes these parts.

#1 — Making a commitment

When you are striving to achieve, commitment takes on a whole different meaning. I have seen more commitments broken than commitments kept. This seems to be average behavior within our society.

The foundation for winning behavior is keeping your commitments. High achievers, however, act differently. They develop what I call a "winning behavior," and the foundation for winning behavior is this: *keeping commitments*. It is evident by their habit of always doing what they say they are going to do.

When you choose to be accountable to your goals, you must:

A) make a commitment to perform the KPIs at a level you can perform and

B) report on that performance weekly to a mentor or a group of like-minded people.

Performing at benchmark, in the beginning, is not the most important issue. The most important issue is to **do what you say you are going to do.** The difference between what you say and what you do is called your **performance gap.**

**Your objective is to do what you say
and consistently increase your performance
until you reach benchmark.**

The time it takes you to get to benchmark is completely up to you.

I have used this affirmation for years regarding commitment:
"A commitment made is a debt unpaid until delivered."

Some people make commitments and then decide if they are really going to follow through. For me, a commitment made is like owing money, and I have signed the note! I cannot forfeit on that commitment any more than I can forfeit on borrowed money.

Doing what you say you are going to do is the most important winner behavior you will ever develop, and the choice of accountability helps you develop that behavior.

#2 — Building confidence in your untapped potential

Most people do not develop in grand leaps. Occasionally you will see a top achiever quickly rise to the top, but I have experienced that most of us grow in small increments.

The reality of achievement **is that it does not matter how small the step is, as long as you take those steps consistently and those steps continue to increase.** It is the old grow or decline theory. You must make a commitment to grow consistently and never settle into a no-growth pattern.

Consistent growth requires confidence, and confidence only comes from the experience of successful attempts. **There is no better place to experience successful attempts than in the choice of accountability.**

> **Consistent growth requires confidence, and confidence only comes from the experience of successful attempts.**

When you choose accountability, you must make a commitment to do what you say you are going to do and report on that to an outside partner on a weekly basis. During this process you will experience success and failure. It becomes a weekly proving ground for your commitment.

As you learn from this weekly choice of accountability, you begin to notice that you are doing things that you never thought possible. With time, you begin to understand this truth:

**You possess
an unlimited
amount of untapped
potential!**

When you become aware of this untapped potential, you begin to develop confidence in your potential. You become aware that no matter how challenging the future may be, you have the untapped potential to successfully deal with it.

It is difficult, if not impossible, to develop this confidence in your untapped potential *without* choosing to be accountable to your goals and learning to make a commitment.

#3 — Understand that accountability is a choice

Accountability is a mature choice. Some say that accountability is a sign of weakness. These people try to achieve in private with a false sense of independence and pride. They may reason, "I only need me, and I can account for myself better than anyone."

The choice of accountability is usually the most significant choice anyone can make regarding their future achievement.

I have known only a few people who could do this on their own, and I would never recommend it. **For all next-level growth and every next-level step I have made in my life, the choice of accountability played a major role.**

Most of us need the outside perspective of accountability to grow, and in most cases, no one can make that choice for you. Forced accountability will produce only temporary results.

Choosing accountability is an effective choice because you cannot hide behind your comfort zones. Accountability **pushes you past those self-imposed limitations** and **into a lifestyle of achievement and growth**, which is what you want!

When you step forward with the choice of accountability, you are saying YES to achievement and growth.

Notes to Self:

_____

_____

_____

_____

_____

_____

_____

_____

_____

_____

_____

_____

_____

_____

_____

_____

_____

_____

_____

PART II

PART II

USING A PROVEN SYSTEM TO SUCCEED

We have devoted the first half of this book to the discussion of learning to make effective choices. You are therefore aware that the management of effective, daily choices like positive attitude, effective actions, and the choice of accountability, are not natural responses.

In order to be consistently effective, you must have ...

**a consistent system,
exclusive of your own instincts,
to manage your daily choices and actions.**

The remaining chapters are intended to serve as your personal guide to the Next-Level Achievement System®.

CHAPTER FIVE

THE NEXT-LEVEL ACHIEVEMENT SYSTEM®

In this chapter, we will begin building the foundation of an effective personal management system. For over 20 years, I have personally used and helped thousands of leaders learn an effective system that I call the Next-Level Achievement System®.

Regardless of what you may be thinking, please approach this system with an open mind. It is time proven, and it works incredibly well. You have my word on that!

There is only one purpose for this Next-Level Achievement System® ... **to bypass your natural, human instincts.**

Remember:

> **Your human instincts
> are only interested
> in your comfort and safety,
> and their #1 goal is to keep you
> where you are.**

That is why change is usually uncomfortable.

55

When you develop and use a system that is designed to keep you focused on what matters most, you *bypass* those **nagging comfort zones** and **systematically move toward goal-directed achievement.**

Fighting change

Have you ever attended an inspirational or motivational event and come away with great intentions to change, only to find yourself back to your old habits within just a few days?

Every year, fitness centers across the US are overwhelmed by new registrations in January from people who genuinely want to become physically fit. They have good intentions that are backed by New Year's resolutions, but by March, most of these new registrations have cancelled.

Old habits do not just go away ... you must displace them.

Why are good intentions not enough to generate change?

Good intentions must be supported by effective choices, and that is where most people go astray. Achievement happens moment by moment, one day at a time! Many people have difficulty translating their good intentions into goal-directed, daily choices and actions. They don't realize this truth:

**Good intentions are
under the direct control
of your natural, human instincts.**

Without an effective management system, which keeps your choices in alignment with your goals, **your comfort zones and habits of thought will take over.** That is why a personal management system is vital in achievement.

You cannot become who you have never been by doing what you have always done. Positive change is the key to achievement, and your effective daily choices are the stepping stones.

The 4 elements of the Next-Level Achievement System®

Simplicity is the key to a successful system of achievement for any leader because a simple system can be duplicated by others. Group energy is generated from the use of a common system within any group, large or small. Then, from a consistent system of achievement, a common language and a synergy of teamwork is spawned.

I will briefly discuss each of the elements of the Next-Level Achievement System® here, but the following four chapters will describe each of these elements in greater detail.

ELEMENT #1 — A vision statement

Your vision statement should be less than one page and should be written in present tense. Begin by writing a description of your life 5 to 10 years in the future as if you are already there. You should be somewhat realistic, but be careful not to limit your potential. This statement will be the foundation for all your future planning.

A part of your vision is a statement of your life's mission/purpose. This mission/purpose statement will be remembered monthly in your personal management system. Your mission/purpose statement should describe your best self and define your heart and soul. Be patient, because a good mission/purpose statement may take years of refinement.

ELEMENT #2 — Annual goals

At the beginning of each new year, set 3 to 5 annual goals that will move you closer to your vision. These goals will be, and should always be, determined by and based upon your vision.

From these 3 to 5 goals, you will create action steps that outline what you need to do to accomplish these goals.

ELEMENT #3 — Monthly plans

The action steps from your annual goals should filter down to your monthly plans. You will need a month-at-a-glance calendar for this. All target dates from the action steps of your annual goals, along with all scheduled events, should be entered into your monthly calendar.

ELEMENT #4 — Daily actions

Each day of your monthly plan should transfer to your daily actions, one day at a time. These daily plans will include imperative/important things to do, contacts and follow-ups, and a time schedule of your day.

The key to daily planning is to *always* plan tomorrow before tomorrow begins.

Good intentions must be supported by effective choices. You may be thinking, "Wait, I didn't get all that you said!"

That is fine. The next four chapters will be devoted to explaining in detail each of these parts of the Next-Level Achievement System®.

58

Planning is required

Achievement happens moment by moment, one day at a time! Effective daily choices come from a systems approach to pre-planning and daily management. **Becoming a master of daily planning is also a significant winner behavior you must develop.**

One of the most commonly asked questions that I get from clients is, "How can I achieve and still maintain balance in my life?"

We want to have it all, but can you have it all and still be balanced? I believe that a balanced life of abundance is achievable. My consistent answer to this question is, "**You can have it all if you commit to becoming a master planner!**"
Here it is:

A) If you want abundance, then you must have achievement and balance, and

B) If you want achievement and balance, then you must have a system of personal management that consistently brings your focus to the moment-by-moment, one-day-at-a-time process of effective actions.

Quite simply, you cannot have abundance without your system of personal management.

To grow, you must overcome ineffective behaviors, and that requires the implementation of new, more effective behaviors. **Replacing old habits with new habits requires a system that stimulates behavior change.**

59

And again, behavior change *without* an external, consistent system would be difficult, if not impossible.

The desired personal habit of daily management is to plan first and act second.

**You should always have
your monthly plan ready
before the month begins —
and your daily plan ready
before each day begins.**

Prior planning helps you to become proactive against the comfort zone of procrastination. **Comfort zones rush in to fill the vacuum left by unplanned months and days.** Your system keeps you goal directed by pre-planning, and you simply act **rather than renegotiate** with your comfort zones.

As soon as you retreat to an old comfort zone for rest, you lose momentum. Your best plans and intentions are worthless unless you assume personal **responsibility and develop the capacity to mange your effective choices.** In other words, simply do what you plan to do without hesitancy, regardless of circumstances or what other people say, think, or do.

Notes to Self:

_____

_____

_____

_____

_____

_____

_____

_____

_____

_____

_____

_____

_____

_____

_____

_____

_____

_____

_____

_____

_____

CHAPTER SIX

THE VISION STATEMENT

Clarity creates focus! The clearer the vision (mental picture) of your future, the more focused your daily activities will be.

Maintaining consistent, **daily focus is vital for achievement**, and focus is a significant factor in the **sustainability** of that achievement.

Riding the wave up ... and then down?

It is not uncommon to watch someone achieve a level of great success, only to see them decline shortly thereafter. Why is that?

The answer to that question goes back to the basic problem we all have with achievement — **comfort zones** designed and built by our natural, human instincts.

After we reach a new level of achievement, there is a tendency to revert to our comfort zones. We rationalize this behavior by saying, "I just need a break." **The real meaning** of that comment is, "I am so far from my comfort zone that I choose to go back there for awhile."

There is absolutely nothing wrong with a well-planned break for rest and to re-energize. However,

a WELL-PLANNED BREAK
vs.
a RETREAT TO AN OLD COMFORT ZONE
are two completely
different
issues!

The danger of retreating to old comfort zones is that you cannot sustain consistent growth by going back to old habits and behaviors. As soon as you retreat to an old comfort zone for rest, you lose momentum. **This dysfunction is caused by lack of focus.** **Prior planning helps you to become proactive against the comfort zone of procrastination.**

With clear focus, a well-planned break can propel you to higher achievement. But that is not the same as dropping back to a comfort zone of "no-growth."

The instant you revert to old habits and comfort zones, all growth stops, and as you know, there are only two growth choices in life: grow or decline!

The value of vision

Our human design includes a unique and creative gift ... **the gift of imagination.** We are the only part of creation with this unique gift. The ability to use our imagination to **envision a future as you want it to be** is the key to daily focus.

When you allow yourself to use your imagination to picture a future as you want it to be ...

    a) you create clarity,

    b) and future clarity

    c) creates focus for the moment.

This is why I place vision at the very beginning of my work with clients. The Next-Level Achievement System® rests on vision as the cornerstone of the entire foundation for the system.

Some of us have been conditioned by culture and education to believe that the use of our imaginations is an **inferior** and **wasteful** form of thinking. I remember several well-meaning but ill-informed teachers in my childhood who told me, "Stop daydreaming and pay attention."

From this all-too-common type of negative conditioning, we develop resistance to the use of our imagination. We begin to think of daydreaming as wasteful.

In fact, the act of considering your vision as a process can actually be painful for certain personality types. Those who can only believe in what exists as current reality will say things like, "I believe in what I can see or touch." As a result, they have an additional resistance to an appreciation of imagination as a significant and creative thinking process.

Is that you? If so, I suggest that you change your thinking about the gift of imagination.

Over the years, I have experienced all types of resistance to the process of vision, but the beneficial effects of using the imagination in the creation of a long-term vision is a significant factor in the system of achievement. **The real value of vision is that it puts the WHY behind what you do!**

Building a vision statement

I find that the most common practice of building vision is to simply list the things you may want in your future. A list of future wants is a good place to start, but that is a "Dream List," and I will cover that in the next chapter on goals.

A meaningful vision statement is much more than just a list of future wants. **A passionate vision statement actually propels you into your future with a vivid mental picture that includes sights, sounds, colors, feelings, and emotions.**

A well-prepared vision statement will inspire both your feelings and your emotions.

STEP #1 — Pick a date in the future

The best way to get started building your own vision statement is to pick a future date (many people choose their birthday) five years into the future.

Your vision statement is never about reality; it's about designing life by your dreams.

Now, with that date in mind, write down all the facts that would relate to your life at that time, such as your age, ages of the members of your family, home, location, or activities.

STEP #2 — Define your future

Next, think about the future facts and relate those facts to fit exactly what you want your life to look like in five years. You are defining your future as you want it to be.

STEP #3 — Write it out

Once you have your thoughts in place, write a narrative description of a day in your life, five years into your future. Design your narrative exactly as you want it to be.

Here is the key: **Write your narrative in the present tense as if you are already there.**

Your vision statement should be no more than one page long and should evoke strong feelings and emotions when you read it. There is something about building your vision statement into a description of a day in your life that brings your vision to life with all the sights, sounds, and feelings of reality.

STEP #4 — Post it so you can read it often

When you have your vision statement ready, type it up on your computer and put it into a format that you want. Then frame it and place it in a location where you will see it often.

Remember that your vision statement is never about reality. It is about designing life by your dreams. You only have two choices regarding your future:

**You can plan it
the way you want it to be,
or you can wait for the situations
and circumstances of life
to design it for you.**

Your vision statement should grow as you grow. Every year you will review your vision statement and update it as you see fit. **Your evaluation should always be how compelling your vision is, not how realistic it is.**

66

In the next chapter, you will learn how you can derive your annual goals, which will be very specific, measurable, and realistic, from your vision statement.

Every year, you will ask yourself, "What can I accomplish this year that will move me closer to my vision?"

That is how specific annual goals act as stepping-stones to your vision of tomorrow.

The power of vision

Long-term vision is the key to energy, focus, and consistency. Clarity of vision acts as a magnet, **for you attract to yourself that which you set out for yourself.**

With clear vision, you can recognize opportunity when it presents itself because it fits the vision that you have carefully designed and clearly pictured for your future.

Without vision, people become:

    listless,
        restless,
            scattered,
                fearful,
                    pessimistic,
                        negative,
    judgmental,
        short-sighted,
            burned-out,
                frustrated,
        one-sided,
            unbalanced,
                depressed, and
                    discouraged.

That is a pretty sad list, but it describes many of our friends, family, and acquaintances.

I have experienced each of these dysfunctions with past clients, but I have also experienced many of those clients enthusiastically declare that clarity of vision was the key to their process of pushing past their mental dilemma.

Get started and stop worrying about how perfect it will be. Solomon said that, "Without vision people perish," and I have observed this to be true. I have numerous examples that prove him right. I have found that almost every case of executive burnout can be resolved with a process of building a passionate vision of the executive's future!

Vision is the foundation of the Next-Level Achievement System®. **You will never regret the time and energy invested in building a passionate vision of your future.** It is not easy, but it is not impossible.

Get started and stop worrying about how perfect it will be. Life is not about perfection — **life is about progress.** Building a passionate, compelling vision statement is one of the most significant requirements of next-level growth.

Notes to Self:

_____
_____
_____
_____
_____
_____
_____
_____
_____
_____
_____
_____
_____
_____
_____
_____
_____
_____
_____
_____
_____

CHAPTER SEVEN

THE GOALS

I remember my mentor, Paul J. Meyer, saying, "If you're not achieving at the level you want, it is simply because your goals are not clearly defined." He always focused on achieving goals, not just setting them, and he insisted that the difference was in the process.

Anyone can set a goal, but **achieving the goal** is the true purpose of goal setting.

Set only a few big goals every year

"The Goals" section here is the second part of the Next-Level Achievement System®. Clearly defined goals serve as your directional compass and drive your effective actions and choices during the year. **Goals turn dreams into reality in small, annual increments.**

Each new year, you need to set specific, realistic annual goals. Those goals are always directed from your vision and dreams.

Begin by asking yourself, "**What specific goals can I achieve this year that will move me closer to my vision and dreams?**"

I recommend that you limit your goals to 1 to 5 big annual goals. The reason I suggest a limit is that the process will require a plan of action for each goal, and the tracking process required is quite involved. Too many goals will distract your focus from the achievement of the most important goals.

As an example, I once had a meeting with a CEO of a major organization. At the beginning of our conversation he said, "**I don't believe our company has a need for any further organizational planning because in three annual planning meetings, our team has established 152 corporate initiatives for the year!**" He beamed with pride.

We proceeded to discuss other issues, but during my remaining time with him, I was thinking to myself:

**"This well-intentioned leader
is totally unaware
of what he has done
to his leadership team."**

He was treating a glorified to-do list as if the 152 corporate initiatives were strategic goals. With this mind-set ...

**he had inadvertently set a
SELF-DEFEATING path of frustration
and a WASTED YEAR
of non-goal-directed work.**

Don't let that be you!

What happened to my goals?

My experience with leaders like this is that they tend to overwhelm their leadership teams with to-do's and call them goals. At the end of the year, they make excuses for why they did not hit the "goals" and set almost the same "goals" again for the next year.

What they are missing are the **clearly defined big goals that will move them closer** to their long-term vision.

In the absence of the clearly defined goal, **initiatives lose their meaning and significance.** Organizational leaders cannot maintain consistent daily focus on vague, undefined initiatives — and neither can you!

So, the initiatives lose their importance, and the function of simply **being busy begins to occupy the focus** of the entire organization. I have noticed that this happens to individual clients as well.

Willingness to work hard is important, but hard work alone does not necessarily lead to achievement.
Remember this:

> **"It's not how much you do,**
> **but the effectiveness of**
> **WHAT you do**
> **that truly counts!"**

Laser focus on specific, predetermined annual goals is the only path to effective work.

Real goals represent those few and specific, all-inclusive, important, annual achievements necessary for consistent progress toward your long-term vision and dreams. The "strategic initiatives" that seem to occupy traditional corporate thinking are usually the **action steps** to the big goals.

But goals are not action steps!

IDENTIFYING real goals and ...

   RECOGNIZING the differences between goals
   and action steps ...

      are the MAGIC INGREDIENTS ...

         to the process of successful goals
         achievement.

I would recommend that you re-read those words several times to let this truth settle in. Most people, including CEOs, do not recognize this important truth.

Identifying your goals

From my past years of experience and observation, I am now convinced that **there is a simple reason** why most people do NOT achieve the goals they set. **Are you ready for it?**

It is simply because ...

      people tend to set goals
      that they really
      do NOT want
      to achieve.

Anytime I use that comment in a group setting, I see both **shock** and **disagreement** in the faces of my audience. The obvious question in their demeanor is, **"How can you say that people set goals that they don't want to achieve?"**

Well, here are two examples to which I believe everyone can relate:

First, have you ever set a New Year's resolution? It feels so good when you do it. It even brings a fresh newness to life and a genuine feeling of beginning anew. That is ... for about a week. Your behaviors never change to come in alignment with your goal, and by March, you say to yourself, "I'll get around to that next year."

Second, have you ever set a weight loss goal? Did you achieve that goal? Now I know that some of you can answer that question with a resounding affirmative, but the majority of people who set weight loss goals never achieve them. Why is that?

The answer to both the failed New Year's resolutions and the unattained weight loss goals is the same:

Your behaviors
NEVER CHANGED
to come in alignment
with your goal!

Ouch! A good measure of reality sometimes hurts. But learn from your lessons so you can avoid repeating the same mistakes.

Here is why: Any time you set a goal and your behavior does not change to come in alignment with the appropriate actions necessary to accomplish the goal, **you have psychologically determined that you do not want to achieve that goal.** And once you subconsciously decide that you do not want what the goal represents, regardless of the work effort, **you will not accomplish the goal.**

This is why identifying the appropriate goal is so important.

In the first part of the Next-Level Achievement System®, you started the goal setting process with the building of your long-term vision. **A clear mental picture of your ideal future is the first step in goal setting.**

Another necessary part of identifying appropriate goals is the building of a Dream List, which is a list of all the things that you ever wanted to have, do, be, and all the places you ever wanted to go. **Dreams are not goals, but they are the beginning of goals.**

Nobody can maintain consistent daily focus on vague, undefined goals.

We do not have room here to write your list, so take a notepad and begin to write down everything that comes to mind.

As you build your list, try not to be judgmental about whether the dream is realistic. If it is in your head as a want, write it down. This will be an ongoing list, hopefully for the rest of your life. Continue to add to your list as often as you think of new dreams, and put a date beside each dream as you write it down.

When I was moving to my new office in July of 2000, after being named President of Leadership Management, Inc. (I began with this company as a young man in 1978), I came across my old Dream List. I had to smile when I looked at #2 on my list from that year: "To become the President of Leadership Management, Inc."

A Dream List has a special, magnetic pull ...

**It seems that you have a tendency
to attract to yourself
that which you
set out for yourself.**

75

Lastly, keep updating your list of dreams. It is an important part of identifying your goals.

Where the goal setting process begins

The best time to set goals is the first of the year, but getting started is the most important step. So, get started now, regardless of the time of year. Then plan to use the last quarter of every year to establish your goals for the next year.

Here is where the goal setting process begins:

#1 — Review your vision statement

As you begin, start with a review of your vision statement. Your review should be about how compelling it is. If it has lost some of its luster, refine it. Your vision statement should grow as you grow.

#2 — Read through your Dream List

After you review your vision, read through your Dream List. Now ask yourself, "What can I accomplish this year that will bring me closer to my vision and dreams?"

The answers to this question are the beginning of your annual goals program.

#3 — Choose your top goals

As you write down the things you want to accomplish this year, try to identify which of those things are primary and which things are systemic. In other words, decide which things are the primary goals and which things are the results of the accomplishment of the primary goals.

As an example, say you wrote down these three things as goals for the year:

1. Earn $70,000 income
2. Increase savings account by $8,000
3. Buy a new home

On the surface, this list looks like three separate goals, but in reality, the list represents **one primary goal** and **two systemic benefits.** All three things are related to the financial area of your life and without the income of $70,000, the savings increase and the new home purchase are in jeopardy.

Be honest with yourself: *Are you pursuing a goal that you really do not want to achieve?*

So, what you have is the one goal to earn $70,000 income and the increased savings and new home purchase are two benefits to be gained by reaching your goal.

Identifying the real goal is very important. By identifying the right goals, you can now work on your action plan with confidence.

Taking action on your goals

Once you have set the goals you want to pursue, deciding on your top goals, it is time to put an action plan together. The action plan is the lifeblood of goal setting, for **a goal without an action plan is merely a wish!**

There are three parts to the action plan:

PART #1 — Benefits to be gained and losses to be avoided

77

Write down all the personal benefits that the accomplishment of the goal represents to you.

Once you subconsciously decide that you do not want what the goal represents, regardless of the work effort, you will not accomplish the goal.

Next, ask yourself, "In the pursuit of this goal, are there any losses that I need to avoid?" As an example, if you set a financial goal, you may wish to avoid the loss of relationships or integrity.

People are usually motivated by either the **benefits to be gained** or **losses to be avoided**. It is important to go through the thinking process regarding these two considerations and record them with the statement of the goal.

PART #2 — Obstacles and solutions

There are obstacles to every goal you set, so identify as many as you can, write them down, and then write a corresponding solution to each obstacle.

You cannot proceed with a goal if you have an obstacle to the goal for which there is no solution. In this case, many times the obstacle replaces the old goal and becomes the new goal.

PART #3 — Specific action steps

Write down each separate action step necessary to the accomplishment of the goal. Make sure that each action step is very specific and not vague.

Each action step must have a target date for its completion, and the target date for each action step must be recorded in the appropriate monthly calendar. This assures that the action steps transfer to your monthly plans.

Your goals program

As you can see from this chapter, your goals program becomes the guiding directional compass for your year. Annual goals flow into your monthly plans by target dates. The action steps are then brought into action by your daily planning.

There are many nuances to goals achievement, but they are too numerous to cover here. However, I would like you to remember this: **The way to achieve your goals is to follow the Next-Level Achievement System®.**

By following this system, your vision and dreams slowly grow into reality. You move past being a mere goal setter and you become a master goals achiever!

Notes to Self:

_____
_____
_____
_____
_____
_____
_____
_____
_____
_____
_____
_____
_____
_____
_____
_____
_____
_____
_____
_____
_____
_____

CHAPTER EIGHT

THE MONTHLY PLANS

People often ask me, "How should I remind myself of my goals after I've set them?"

I believe the stimulus for this question relates to the old adage, "**Out of sight, out of mind.**" They are concerned, and rightfully so, that they will forget very quickly if they put their goals program aside and never refer to it during the year.

Keep goals in sight

This mistake has been demonstrated in my personal experiences with major corporations. I have watched organizations pay thousands of dollars for outside management consulting firms to design strategic plans.

Then when all the work is done, the leadership **places the plan on the shelf** and **only refers to it at the end of the next year** to see how close or far they came to the goals!

You can probably guess the results.

You cannot hit goals in the dark. Goals require plans and plans must become relevant on a monthly basis.

In order to remember your goals on a consistent basis:

> **Your goals must have action steps**
> **and those action steps**
> **must flow, systematically,**
> **into monthly plans.**

In addition:

> **The target dates for the action steps**
> **must stand out as a**
> **time-scheduled event on**
> **the appropriate monthly calendar.**

This is accomplished by the systematic process of monthly planning.

The purposes of monthly planning

Monthly planning has three purposes:

1) **To remind** yourself of "Who you are" with a Mission/Purpose statement that describes your very heart and soul,

2) **To identify** your top priorities for the month, and

3) **To organize** your time-scheduled events on a monthly calendar so that you can see it at a glance.

We will cover each of these purposes with the appropriate detail needed for you to implement effective monthly planning.

PURPOSE #1 — *Mission/purpose statement*

With corporate clients, I usually suggest the separation of the Vision, Purpose, and Mission as stand-alone statements representing the entire organization. But with individuals, I suggest combining the mission/purpose statements together.

Everyone should have a written mission/purpose statement. **The reason is that we all need to know, with complete clarity, WHO we are!**

If I were to ask you to tell me, in one sentence, who you are, **what would you say?**

Inevitably, people usually respond with a glowing advertisement about what they do ...

BUT there should be

a DISTINCTIVE difference

between WHO you are and

WHAT you do.

That is the very objective of an individual mission/purpose statement. The statement is a one-sentence declaration of who you are and should describe your very heart and soul.

A goal without an action plan is merely a wish.

I have found that good mission/purpose statements never just happen — they usually evolve over time.

Begin by writing a one sentence statement declaring who you are. The best way to do this is to begin the sentence with the words "I am" and simply complete the sentence.

Your mission/purpose statement is for you and should declare who you are rather than what you do. It is not an advertisement for your services. Keep it about who you are not what you do.

As example, "I am an inspiring, caring and compassionate person" is a mission/purpose statement from one of my clients. The objective here is to keep it simple, a clear declaration of who you are.

Mission/Purpose Statement:
(I am ...)

_____

_____

_____

_____

Even though it is only one sentence, this is some of the hardest work you will do. Just get started, and it will evolve into the real you as you remind yourself of your mission/purpose at the beginning of every month.

PURPOSE #2 — Identify monthly priorities

From the last chapter, you learned that the system leads you to clearly defined annual goals. Those goals have specific action plans with target dates, and those target dates are transferred to the appropriate monthly calendar.

Monthly priorities, then, are determined by the action plans and target dates that you establish.

In monthly planning, it is important for you to consider both personal and business priorities for the month. Ask yourself, "What important personal objectives do I have for this month?"

Too many people limit their planning to business only. **This practice leads to imbalance in your life.** Attention to both personal and business planning leads to a fulfilling and abundant life.

Often I hear clients make these complaints:

- **I just don't have enough time!**
- **It seems I never catch up!**
- **Work is never ending!**

Here are the facts: **You have as much time as anyone else.** The problem is that you are not planning. Work is taking up all of the available, unplanned time.

There was a writer of management practice who developed a theory about this very thing. His name was Parkinson and he developed "Parkinson's Law," which says,

**"Work will expand
to fill the time available
for its completion."**

There you go — he nailed it!

If you fail to plan both personal and business time, your work **will expand to fill the unplanned time with nothing but work!**

If you want it all with balance between work, family, and all the other areas of your life ...

BECOME

a MASTER

PLANNER!

Now, once you have identified your personal and business objectives for the month, prioritize both lists. Then, from your priorities, select your top one or two personal and business objectives. **These top objectives are your priorities for the month.**

I have noticed that prioritization is difficult for high achievers because high achievers want everything to be a #1, top priority. As a result, **they overwhelm themselves with too many #1 activities, and they lose focus,** which eventually leads to burnout and frustration.

You cannot hit goals in the dark.

Prioritization is important. Something has to be number #1 something has to be #2, and so on. **Prioritization brings clarity, and clarity creates focus.**

By identifying priorities, it does not mean that you forget all the other monthly objectives. In fact, I suggest that you review your list weekly. But, prioritization does help you focus on those high payoff activities that propel you forward.

From your priorities, write down those activities that hold the highest degree of payoff for you this month. Your monthly objective is to spend the majority of your time in your high payoff activities.

PURPOSE #3 — *Organize your monthly calendar*

Your monthly calendar is the place where you enter all time-scheduled events. It is important to **build the habit** of going directly to your monthly calendar anytime you need to schedule an event that has a date and time.

The reason I suggest this habit is to eliminate the possibility of double entry of a scheduled event and missing an important date. If you enter time-scheduled events in more than one place, such as a legal pad, journal, sticky notes, phone, computer, and a calendar, you will miss a scheduled date from the double entry. Build the habit of entering your time-scheduled dates in one place — your calendar.

At the beginning of each month, **make sure you fill in your entire schedule**, including work, personal, and family time. Review your calendar with others who need to know your schedule before the month begins.

This avoids conflicts of scheduling that come from lack of prior planning.

The #1 rule for monthly planning

You always plan next month before next month begins! Planning next month is a time-scheduled event at the end of each month. Professionals who develop this habit avoid the end-of-the-month syndrome.

The end-of-the-month syndrome goes something like this:

You do 70% - 80%
of your most effective work
after the 15ᵗʰ of the month.

The reason for this habit is that you have designed a comfort zone of retreat at the beginning of each month where you tell yourself, "I have plenty of time."

Prior planning brings clarity, and clarity creates focus.

In your first-of-the-month comfort zone, you are ineffective due to your lack of focus, and that comes from lack of planning. **Remember, clarity creates focus!**

You probably have great plans for achievement, so as the 15th of the month approaches, you step up your activity. In a frantic flurry of activity, you desperately attempt to get a full month's work done in only 10 - 15 days.

Clients complain to me all the time, "I don't know why I do this to myself!"

The answer is this:

> **They have developed**
> **an end-of-the-month**
> **SYNDROME**
> **from a first-of-the month**
> **COMFORT ZONE.**

If that applies to you, it is time to change that.

Monthly planning is one of the cornerstones in the Next-Level Achievement System®. **Planning next month before next month begins** can change your life and your results.

Notes to Self:

_____
_____
_____
_____
_____
_____
_____
_____
_____
_____
_____
_____
_____
_____
_____
_____
_____
_____

CHAPTER NINE

THE DAILY ACTIONS & CHOICES

The best way for me to explain the significance of daily choices and actions is to use an analogy.

Consider an automobile — not just any auto, but picture your favorite make and model. Imagine the new, shiny glow of the metallic color, the new car smell that envelopes you when you sit in the driver's seat, and the engine that purrs and revs with power.

Everything is perfect about this new car of yours except one thing: There are no wheels!

Well, maybe you can justify being happy with what you do have. I mean, the car is beautiful with its shiny color, it has a big powerful engine, and you cannot forget the new car smell.

No, it just will not work, will it? All the benefits are for naught. Why?

For the obvious reason: The wheels are the strategic part of the car that allows it to actually go places!

Your daily actions and choices **represent that strategic part** of the Next-Level Achievement System® that allows you to actually achieve and go places.

In short, your daily actions and choices are the wheels of your life!

You can talk the talk,

> **look the part,**

>> **have all the trappings,**

>>> **project the image,**

and all the things we do to keep from facing reality, **but if you do not do the right things consistently,** your system is unsustainable.

The power and freedom to choose

The power of choice is the very foundation of achievement. The quality of your daily choices and actions are **measured by their effectiveness.**

Daily planning is **the key** to how effective your choices and actions will be.

Dreams transform into reality **in small, sometimes unrecognizable increments.** To achieve and to make that achievement sustainable, you must build the habit of consistent daily planning. You have been blessed with the significant power and freedom to choose. Those goal-directed, consistent, daily choices are the **stepping-stones to your future.**

Always plan tomorrow before tomorrow begins

I believe the most effective choice you will ever develop is that of **planning your tomorrow before tomorrow begins.** This may seem like advice you heard as a child, but I am amazed **how few people** actually do it.

Many people have developed the habit of managing their daily routine by circumstance, situations, or ineffective activities. **They are being led instead of leading.**

For example, they start the work day by waiting for the first thing to happen. They do not know exactly what that will be, but **they assume** that something will **happen because it always does.** From that first circumstance, they move to the next thing, maybe a call, text, or email. But if nothing happens right away, they move on to a familiar and comfortable activity, like listening to some good music or surfing the internet, until something happens.

Always plan next month before the month begins.

With this behavior, they complete their day with **ineffective results** related to their overall achievement.

Recognize the important fact:

> **This reactive style of daily management becomes a comfort zone and breaking that habit can be difficult.**

Planning tomorrow before tomorrow begins is the most effective way to overcome this reactive style of personal management.

Before the end of your day, take 10 minutes to plan tomorrow.
There are three steps involved in planning tomorrow:

STEP #1 — Transfer forward

Transfer any action step, contact, or follow-up that has not
been completed today over to tomorrow's action steps list.
Incomplete action steps should always transfer forward to the
next day until complete.

This habit will prompt you to get things done today because
you know that you will have to transfer it to tomorrow.

STEP #2 — Make notes

Make a permanent note of any communication you need to
pass on to others and the people with whom you need to
communicate that information.

This frees your mind from the task of remembering, **which is
a waste of the creative thought process.** You learn to maxi-
mize face time and phone time.

Simply remember to refer to your notes for the reminder of
what you need to communicate every time you are with
someone, in person or on the phone.

STEP #3 — Stay on schedule

Look at your monthly calendar and transfer your time-scheduled events from your calendar to your daily time plan. This
simply keeps you on schedule.

If you are not in the habit of planning tomorrow before tomorrow begins, it will take some extra work and focus on your part. **Prior planning brings clarity, and clarity creates focus.** Prior planning and clarity are also necessities for success in any endeavor!

Effective habits enhance performance, and planning tomorrow before tomorrow begins is the most effective habit you will ever develop.

Work your daily plan with an effective management tool

Whether you prefer to use manual planners or electronic tools, **the most important thing is that you use something rather than your memory.**

Our brains are most useful when we are being creative and solving problems, but when we use our brains for remembering important bits of information, such as when and where to go, we have rendered this vital resource less than effective.

Your daily management tool needs to be effective at reminding you of your schedule throughout your day.

> **If you use a manual planner,**
> **you must keep it with you**
> **at all times and allow it**
> **to guide you through your day.**

When you are at your desk, on the phone, or in a meeting, develop the habit of keeping the planner open in front of you as a stimulus to stay on time.

I have always used a manual planner simply because I find that writing stimulates clarity of thought and clarity of thought motivates action. I have not experienced that with electronic tools.

However, if you choose to use an electronic tool, make sure it does the following:

1) Allows you to track daily action steps along with your daily time schedule.

2) Allows you to transfer incomplete action steps to the next day, until completed.

3) Allows you to defer things to remember to tell others to a permanent place to remember for you. You want to free your thinking from too many things to remember

You have as much time as anyone else to reach your goals.

Successfully managing your daily choices and actions is dependent upon managing from a plan and not your natural instincts. Using an effective management tool **frees you** to simply work from your plan and **not renegotiate daily** with your habits and comfort zones.

Building effective habits of achievement

Daily management of your effective habits is the key to doing the right things consistently over a sustained period of time.

However:

We naturally build daily habits around our comfort zones.

If you look at your day, you will notice certain habits that are productive — and you will see habits that make almost no contribution to your future achievement.

Achievement requires growth, and growth requires change. You may readily accept that, but recognize this:

**Change will upset
your comfort zones,
and those habits
will fight your growth
every step of the way.**

I have clients ask me, "What should I do with these comfort zones that have grown into habits that are so hard to change?"

My answer is to "displace" the old habits, one at a time.

Displacement is a psychological term that references the replacement of an established habit for a more effective one. Old habits will NOT just go away. **You must push in the new habit to displace the old.** It is like changing a glass of dirty water with clean water. You simply continue pouring the clean water into the glass of dirty water until the old, dirty water is displaced with clean water.

If you fail to plan both personal and business time, your work will expand to fill the unplanned time with nothing but work!

When you begin to implement some of these suggested habits of achievement, **you will be successful by continuously pouring on the new habit.** Every time you catch yourself off the system, **immediately** go back to your new, more effective habit.

Avoid going through the process of feeling bad or feelings of failure. Those thinking patterns are counterproductive to your progress. Just smile and go right back to the new habit.

Rest assured that these effective daily habits can be successfully implemented through the process of displacement within a very short period of weeks.

The effective choices and actions necessary for achievement come to us moment by moment, one day at a time. You cannot manage your daily routine instinctively without your instincts stepping in to protect you or guide you to an old comfort zone.

> **Effective, daily management**
> **must flow from**
> **a system**
> **that is based**
> **on YOUR long-term**
> **dreams and goals.**

The power of choice is a double-edged sword; it cuts both ways. Your daily choices will either **serve your natural instincts of habit and comfort** — or **serve your desire for achievement.**

Gain control of your daily choices and actions, work to make them as effective as you possibly can, and you take control of your achievement and destiny.

Notes to Self:

_____

_____

_____

_____

_____

_____

_____

_____

_____

_____

_____

_____

_____

_____

_____

_____

_____

_____

_____

_____

_____

CHAPTER TEN

WHAT'S MORE

Years ago, in a private conversation, I had a noted author of management theory tell me his definition of "systems thinking." Here is what he said:

> **Systems thinking is demonstrated by mentally climbing above the fray of operations and looking at the entire system as a whole, while at the same time seeing all the individual parts in complete concert.**

I will never forget that definition because it parallels precisely the Next-Level Achievement System®. At the very foundation of the "whole" system are the "individual parts in complete concert."

Achievement is simply **doing the right things consistently over a sustained period of time.**

The "sustained period of time" comes to you moment by moment, one day at a time. **The quality of your daily choices and actions are measured by their effectiveness, and it is the quality of that effectiveness that determines the degree of your achievement.**

Highly effective leaders achieve greatly while ineffective leaders deliver sporadic results and low quality achievement. The difference between these two groups is this:

the consistent

effectiveness

of their actions.

We have discussed the significance of a system of achievement, a system that buffers and separates your human instincts from the management of your process of achievement. Building this system requires a development process rather than just the accumulation of knowledge. Skill and performance are knowledge-based, while achievement and next-level growth are process-based.

The quality of your process determines the quality of your performance.

The seminar industry is filled with those who claim to improve performance levels. They approach this methodology with knowledge-based skills training, but it is my professional opinion, from over 30 years of experience, that **knowledge-based skills training without a proven development process is wasteful and ill-advised.**

You always have to remember:

**Performance quality
is directly related
to the quality
of the process.**

Skills training and a development process are NOT one and the same, as is evidenced by this fact that:

**Training is event-driven
while development is process-driven.**

Furthermore:

**Training is usually aimed at performance,
but development is aimed at the very core
of your process: your habits,
behaviors, conditioning, and comfort zones.**

Achievement is a by-product of the quality of your process, **not your performance.** I know this comment may raise some eyebrows in the human development industry, **but the quality of your process determines the quality of your performance.**

There is certainly a place for training in the enhancement of performance, but not in the absence of a development process.

Let the process you have learned here serve as the stepping-stone to your phenomenal success. And may God bless you and your journey of achievement!

Notes to Self:

_____

_____

_____

_____

_____

_____

_____

_____

_____

_____

_____

_____

_____

_____

_____

_____

_____

_____

_____

_____

_____

PART III

PART III

THE LANGUAGE OF ACHIEVEMENT

Part three of this book is a glossary of words and terms that have demonstrated significance within The Next-Level Achievement System®.

These are the very words and terms with which many of my clients experimented and now use in their "Word for the Day" calls.

CHAPTER ELEVEN

CHANGING LIVES ONE WORD AT A TIME

As a leader, the more you can promote shared context within your organization the **greater the level of awareness development**. This is important because awareness is the beginning of positive change and growth. Increased knowledge does not necessarily lead to positive change.

In other words...

just knowing something does not change anyone.

Knowing is an intellectual level of understanding, while awareness is an experiential level of understanding. When increased knowledge begins to lead to new levels of awareness, you have begun a significant development process.

The "Word for the Day" call is an **effective** way of building shared context around a common, organizational system of individual development. The spaced repetitious learning of how the words fit into the big picture creates new levels of awareness within people who comprise the organization.

People begin to become aware of how the common system will benefit them. I believe that people will always choose to change when they become aware that the change will serve their best interest.

Obviously the "Word for the Day" call is not a stand-alone system of development. It simply serves as one of your tools in creating new levels of awareness. I believe that an effective and comprehensive, development process requires three distinct elements.

1. "Awareness" Development

2. Individual access to a consistent "Personal Management System"

3. Fostering of a positive "Culture"

#1 — Awareness Development

Number one: "Awareness Development" is always the first step for anyone engaged in a development process. "You don't know what you don't know!"

Awareness is the point when you begin to connect the dots between what you know and what you do.

Awareness is the point when you begin to connect the dots between what you know and what you do.

How many people in the world "know" that consistent exercise is a positive health choice? In comparison, how many of those same people continue to choose to say no to a consistent exercise program regardless of that knowledge?

However, when a lifetime of poor health choices leads to undesirable results, the overwhelming, medical knowledge turns into personal awareness of the consequences. That awareness can now begin a life changing transformation. All positive change begins with awareness because awareness leads to new choices.

Any effective development process **must** have a simple, consistent tool for stimulating the consistent development of new levels of awareness.

#2 — Personal Management System

Number two: "A simple, consistent Personal Management System" helps people learn how to manage effective "Choice" on a daily, moment-by-moment basis.

TODAY: You are today the sum total of the choices you have made in your past.

TOMORROW: You will be tomorrow the sum total of the choices you make from this moment forward.

In light of that truth, it would seem logical that the more effective your choices are, the more abundant your achievement becomes.

People need a personal management system that is easy to use and easy to teach others to use. A daily personal management system helps people **move past their natural, human instincts and become proactive** at life rather than instinctively reacting to life.

To understand more about a personal management system I refer you to Part two of this book.

#3 — *Fostering a Positive Culture*

Number three: "Promoting a Positive Culture" must be a proactive process. Culture represents the positive or negative quality of inter-personal support, communications, values, ideologies, behaviors, and relationships that exist within an organization.

As a leader, **you obviously want to develop a positive culture.** Positive culture within an organization can only be developed through a proactive process.

Culture will develop regardless of leadership influence ... but is it the culture you want?

Culture will develop regardless of leadership influence but will most likely turn into a negative, counter-productive culture. Unless influenced by leadership through a positive culture building process the organization turns to the natural, human instincts of each member of the team. Instinctively each team member begins to protect their own turf, ideas, and values, which leads the culture into a negative no growth position.

However, leadership can **proactively drive positive culture** by implementing a consistent process. The Next-Level Achievement System® is designed to instill a positive culture of accountability in which people value commitment, productive activity, achievement, and growth.

The "Word for the Day" call is a small but effective tool that contributes to this accountability culture. Shared context promotes confidence and confidence is the beginning stage of growth.

The "Word for the Day Call" should not be confused with any of the daily inspirational messages to which everyone is accustomed. I love inspirational thought, but a feel-good, rhyming statement has no meaning unless it substantiates "Truth!" So many times I read these daily inspirational messages only to find that, even though the words sound good, the truth of the statement is absent.

Also, the inspirational statement without shared context loses its development capacity because people are interpreting the statement from their own, personal perspective.

Notes to Self:

_____

_____

_____

_____

_____

_____

_____

_____

_____

_____

_____

_____

_____

_____

_____

_____

_____

_____

_____

CHAPTER TWELVE

THE WORDS YOU USE

The following list of words and terms are listed first by number. I discuss the working definitions of each of the words and terms in detail on the pages following the list. The definitions are numbered according to the number on the list. I did this so that you may use this list as a quick reference without thumbing through the pages.

Also, the words and terms are not in alphabetical order for a reason. I have listed the words in order of their position within the Next-Level Achievement System®.

Words and Terms

1. Achievement
2. Next-Level Growth
3. Potential
4. Awareness
5. Change
6. Natural, human instinct
7. Effectiveness
8. Choice
9. Attitude

10. Action
11. Accountability
12. Confidence
13. Personal Management System
14. Vision
15. Master Dream List
16. Goals
17. Monthly Plans
18. Initiatives
19. High Payoff Activities
20. Daily Activity
21. Can Do
22. Perspective
23. Clarity
24. Focus
25. Momentum
26. Emotional Courage
27. Development
28. Process
29. Effective Leadership
30. Effective Activity
31. Effective Perspective
32. Effective Choices
33. Effective Communication
34. Effective Life

1. Achievement:
Doing the right things consistently over a sustained period of time

"Achievement is a by-product of both performance and effectiveness. The process of achievement begins with learning how to manage the effectiveness of your moment-by-moment choices. As the quality of effectiveness increases, the quality of performance improves, which determines the level of your achievement."

2. Next-Level Growth:

Personal growth and development that allows you to achieve at a higher level than you have ever achieved before

"Next-level growth is difficult because it usually requires change, and change is contrary to our natural, human instincts. We instinctively interpret sameness as security. It is this instinctive response that fights next-level growth. Reaching new levels of achievement requires a development process. That process must by-pass your natural, human instincts."

3. Potential:

Those gifts, talents, and determinations of will that lie dormant within each human being

"All human beings have an abundance of untapped potential. Most people use only a small portion of their true potential in a lifetime. Increased performance is dependent upon an effective process designed to develop that untapped potential."

4. Awareness:

The point one reaches when knowledge begins to influence effective behavior

"There is a big difference between knowing something and being aware of something. When you begin to connect the dots between what you know and what you do, you begin to make new choices that are directly related to that new level of awareness."

5. Change:
A proactive move from existing behaviors to more productive, goal-directed choices

"Growth usually requires change; however, change is contrary to our natural, human instincts. That is why we all have problems with change; habits are hard to break, weight is hard to lose, and addictions are hard to break. Change is an inevitable process. Our lives are benchmarked by constant change. The key to managing change is a proactive perspective of positive expectancy toward all change."

6. Natural, human instinct:
The inherent, personal, internal drive for self-preservation

"Self-preservation is the number one goal of our natural, human instincts. We instinctively interpret sameness as security. We instinctively create psychological comfort zones that keep us where we are. We were created to live above our natural, human instincts. We do so by learning how to use the creative gifts of imagination and the power of choice."

7. Effectiveness:
The process of multiplying what works, abandoning what doesn't and always knowing the difference

"Effectiveness is the beginning of all high achievement. It's not how much you do but the effectiveness of what you do that truly counts. Effectiveness is a measureable process. As the measurement of effectiveness increases the quality of your performance improves and with enhanced performance comes higher achievement."

8. Choice:
A proactive or reactive, decision created to perpetuate an existing life position or promote a more productive life position

"We make thousands of choices every day. The quality of our choices determines the degree of our achievement. There is power in our choices. We are today the sum total of the choices of our past. We will be tomorrow the sum total of the choices we make from this point forward. It seems obvious that the more effective our choices the greater our achievement."

9. Attitude:
A proactive or reactive habit of though

"Attitude is a habitual way of thinking. Through our past conditioning those habits of thought may be positive or negative. A positive attitude is usually never instinctive. Instinctively we usually develop negatives attitudes. Instinctively negative attitudes seem more comfortable because they fit our comfort zones of sameness. A positive attitude must be developed. Positive attitudes are built from proactive thought. Looking for the good rather than the bad is a mind-set driven from a pre-determined, positive choice."

10. Action:
Behavior motivated by choice

"We choose our actions every day. Not all actions have the same degree of effectiveness. Instinctively we choose actions that are most comfortable. Learning how to manage the effectiveness of our actions is the key to achievement."

11. Accountability:

A proactive, personal choice to use the power of peer influence to push yourself past your natural, human instincts in order to achieve next-level growth

"The personal choice of accountability is the strongest source of human motivation I have ever witnessed. We resist the choice of accountability because we instinctively desire to stay where we are. The choice of accountability pushes you past your comfort zones and self-imposed limitations."

12. Confidence:

A mental and emotional state of mind created by the experience of successful attempts

"Building new levels of confidence are the beginnings of personal growth. We develop confidence from experiencing successful attempts. Any effective development process must include a systematic and consistent method of allowing people to experience winning. We never learn to win by constantly falling short of the goal. The beginning of confidence is when you recognize where you really are and start there. You can never grow from where you think you should be. You can only grow from where you really are."

13. Personal Management System:

A consistent, proactive method of managing personal choice on a moment-by-moment, one-day-at-a-time basis

"To achieve consistently we need an effective method of pushing past our natural, human instincts. A physical, daily system that is simple to implement is the best way to do that. The system should be based on your dreams and goals and should emphasize proactive planning (Planning tomorrow before tomorrow begins, planning next month before next month begins, and planning next year before next year begins). Having a physical, personal management system that promotes daily proactive behaviors is the key to consistent achievement because it by-passes your natural, human instincts."

14. Vision:
Using the gift of imagination to look into your future and design life as you would like for it to be

"We usually move in the direction of our expectancy. Positive expectancy is a powerful tool when used proactively. Vision is a mental snap-shot picture of what your life looks like in five years. When you use your imagination to envision your future as you would like for it to be, you set in motion the power of expectancy. Vision acts as a compass for your life. It simply gives you the direction to travel. Vision is not a goal, but it provides a magnetic pull that gives you insight into what important goals to set along the way. Each new year you can ask yourself, 'What goals can I accomplish this year that will move me closer to my desired, long-term future.' Without vision people perish!"

15. Master Dream List:
An ongoing master list of everything you have ever wanted to have, to be, to do, or every place you have ever wanted to go

"A dream list is where you take off the 'judge's robe' and let your imagination run free. You should give no thought to how realistic the list is. This is an exercise of the imagination. The dream list adds to your vision by listing everything. The master dream list will never be completed and serves as a 'holding-tank' for future goals."

117

16. Goals:
Specific statements of predetermined, measurable accomplishments, accompanied by specific, measurable action steps and projected target date

"The Next-Level Achievement System® defines goals on an annual basis. Your five year 'Vision' directs the setting of annual 'Goals' that translate into monthly 'Initiatives' and 'High Payoff Activities (HPAs).'Those HPAs determine your daily plans. In the system, your moment-by-moment choices are interconnected all the way up to your long-term vision. By setting annual goals, you can by-pass your natural, human instincts by simply following your personal management system. That is always in your best interest because your system is based on your long-term expectancy for your future."

17. Monthly Plans:
The incremental monthly steps toward annual goals comprised of "Mission Statement," "Initiatives" and "High Payoff Activities"

"You should always plan next month before next month begins. Monthly planning has three purposes, first is to remind yourself of who you are with a mission statement, second is to set priorities, and third is to identify the activities that hold the highest value related to your initiatives."

18. Initiatives:
The predetermined goals/objectives for the month

"In the system we refer to monthly goals/objectives as 'Initiatives.' This is to eliminate confusion and clarify the distinct differences between annual goals and monthly initiatives. I find that people use the word 'Goals' indiscriminately applying the word to anything they may want. It seems best to clarify the differences between annual goals and monthly plans with distinctly different words."

19. *High Payoff Activities:*
Those predetermined actions that are directly related to the accomplishment of your monthly initiatives

"Not all activities have the same value. Instinctively we tend to move toward those activities which are most comfortable. By defining the activities that are directly related to your initiatives and directing your daily actions around those activities, you by-pass your natural, human instincts making your actions more effective."

20. *Daily Activity:*
The choices of action on a moment-by-moment, daily basis

"Consistent achievement comes down to one issue… effective choice! When your daily choices consistently reflect the predetermined activities related to your monthly initiatives, you move to a higher level of effectiveness."

21. *"Can-do":*
Directing your perspective toward the specific things that are under your complete control

"Perspective is the beginning step toward focus and momentum. Perspective is the way you are looking at your life. Most people spend too much time thinking of all the things that they cannot do! If you truly cannot do something, any time invested in that thinking is wasted. To clarify your perspective, first evaluate your current reality. Write down all your thoughts about where you really are. Now, write a list of all the things you can-do, right now, related to your current reality. This process will generate a can-do perspective that will put you in a proactive life position."

22. Perspective:
The emotional/psychological view of one's current reality

"Your perspective is the way you are looking at your current life position. I find that a person's perspective is either positive or negative. There is usually no in-between perspective. It is either proactive or reactive. Perspective can be driven by fear or faith and hope. A proactive, can-do focused perspective is always the most effective."

23. Clarity:
The immediate by-product of an effective perspective

"Clarity is the beginning phase of focus. When your actions are driven by a proactive, can-do perspective you become very clear as to your purpose and actions. Confusion, frustration, and feelings of being overwhelmed come from an ineffective perspective which produces unclear actions."

24. Focus:
The immediate by-product of clarity

"When you become clear as to your current reality and those actions over which you have complete control, you generate focus. Focus is a by-product of clarity. Should you ever lose focus, you must start over with perspective."

25. Momentum:
The immediate by-product of focus

"A proactive, can-do perspective leads to clarity, clarity leads to focus, and momentum is the culmination of that entire process. People believe that momentum is hard to get and easy to lose. It's not if you know how to generate it! Momentum begins with perspective."

26. Emotional Courage:
The conditioned capacity to respond to all life events with positive actions rather than negative beliefs about yourself or your future

"Emotional courage must be developed. None of us are born with this capacity. You develop this capacity through experience and personal development. I find that it is a predetermined mind-set in which you decide to respond to all life events with positive actions. With every adversity lies the seed of an equal or greater benefit."

27. Development:
The process of positive growth

"There is a big difference between training and development. Training deals with knowledge and development deals with behavior change. Both training and development are important. However, training without a development process is unsustainable. Training programs that are changing every 6 months is an indication that the development process is missing."

28. Process:
The proactive steps of development generated by ever increasing levels of awareness

"Development requires process. Process is experiential based while training is knowledge based. As a person experiences new levels of awareness they begin to change behaviors. Behavior change leads to new choices, and all that takes time... that is process."

29. Effective Leadership:
Leadership that consistently creates positive work environments, delivers measurable results, and maintains the ethical integrity of the organization

"Effective leaders believe in the potential of all people and are adept at helping people grow. Effective leaders foster positive growth because they understand the development process. They understand that the development process drives and enhances any training program. Effective leadership is not about making someone feel better, training them harder and longer, taking care of them, or doing someone's work for them. Effective leadership is about one thing... helping people grow!"

30. Effective Activity:
Consistent choices of action that lead to predetermined, positive results

"Effectiveness begins with moment-by-moment choice. Effective activity is driven by those predetermined choices that lead to positive results. Effectiveness can be measured by identifying those activities that are directly related to your desired results. We call those activities High Payoff Activities or HPAs. Once you have identified the HPAs for the month simply measure your effectiveness weekly on a sliding scale of 1 through 10 for each one. An effectiveness score of 70% or more will deliver 90% of all your predetermined initiatives."

31. Effective Perspective:
A proactive emotional and psychological view of the reality of your life that is based on what you can realistically do about that reality

"High achievement flows from a proactive, positive perspective. So many times we become unclear about our life's direction by focusing on all the things that we cannot do. If you can't do something any time spent on thinking about is wasted. When you have a perspective that is based on being clear about your current reality and what you can-do about it, you create clarity and clarity creates focus."

32. Effective Choices:
Those choices that are directly related to ones future dreams and goals

"The power of choice is the determining factor in consistent achievement. Not all choices have the same value. Those choices that are directly related to your desired results are effective choices. You are today the sum total of the choices you have made in your past. You will be tomorrow the sum total of the choices that you make from this moment forward. When you begin to manage effective choice on a moment-by-moment basis, you begin the journey of achievement."

33. Effective Communication:
Communication that is given and received in a manner that accomplishes the original intentions of the communication

"You always communicate! Everything you do communicates something. Communication can be verbal or non-verbal and involves both a sender and a receiver. That communication is either effective or ineffective. Effective communication takes place when the intended message, purpose, and information are both sent and received. Effective communication is the direct responsibility of leadership."

34. Effective Life:
A life of abundance and significance that is sustained by a passion for achievement and driven by long-term vision

"The journey of achievement begins with effectiveness. The degree of your effectiveness determines your performance. The quality of your performance determines the measurement of your achievement, and consistent achievement leads to the by-product of the entire process… Success! Since success is a by-product of the entire process of effectiveness, you would be well served to become a student of that process. You may be surprised to find that, as you become proficient at the process, you will fall in love with the journey not the destination. That is when abundance shows up in your life. The destination of success does not necessarily lead to abundance. However, an effective life is filled with it!"

Notes to Self:

APPENDIX

The following instructions comprise the how-to information given to me by my clients about the implementation of the "Word for the Day" call.

"Word for the Day"

Language consists of words, thoughts, ideas and concepts. We can begin each day by:

1. Choosing one word
2. Reading its definition and explanation
3. Putting it into the context of the Next-Level Achievement System®
4. Creating affirmations surrounding it
5. Using it in our self-talk and communications with others

By having everyone on the same page you can begin to develop a common language. Focusing on a common word each day allows all participants to become adept at the common Language of Achievement. It truly can change lives, one word at a time.

Choose one word every day and do the following:

1. Read about it
2. Write out an affirmation using it

3. Use it in your self-talk and your communication with others

4. Write it on your daily page in your Achievement Planner

Put together a "Master-Mind" group and spend 15 minutes every day sharing the "Word for the Day" on a conference call. Have a new word every day, have someone host the call, and call on several veterans of the language to spend a few minutes sharing the concepts behind that word. The brief sharing of personal stories and insights are very important to the call.

Make sure all the people who are speaking know the "Word for the Day" in advance of the call. Send out a monthly schedule every month to all the speakers. Invite others on to the call to get their days started on a foundation and mindset of achievement. Once a month, have an open-line day and have all the participants share their favorite "Word" and how it has made their life more effective.

Having different speakers and developing new speakers becomes a vital part of the awareness process. You are literally taking knowledge from a level of awareness and ultimately personal growth.

It's amazing how starting your day with a word in shared context can change your thinking and enhance attitudes. You can actually change your life one word at a time.

FROM DAVID BYRD

I sincerely hope that this book may serve as a guide for many who search for that next level in their lives and careers. If you believe that I may be of some help to you in your achievement journey, please contact me at:

davidbyrd@davidbyrdconsulting.com

Next-level growth usually requires an experienced outside-in perspective. I would be honored to share my experiences with you in your journey.

To learn more about what I do and how I help leaders take it to the next level, visit my website:

www.davidbyrdconsulting.com